Need a Hug?

Ceil Golightly Ramsey

Copyright © 2025 by Cecelia Ramsey

All rights reserved. No part of this book may be reproduced or transmitted in any form or by any means, electronic or mechanical, including photocopying, recording, or any information storage and retrieval system, without permission in writing from the author.

ISBN: 978-1-6653-0991-2

This ISBN is the property of BookLogix for the express purpose of sales and distribution of this title. The content of this book is the property of the copyright holder only. BookLogix does not hold any ownership of the content of this book and is not liable in any way for the materials contained within. The views and opinions expressed in this book are the property of the Author/Copyright holder, and do not necessarily reflect those of BookLogix.

∞ This paper meets the requirements of ANSI/NISO Z39.48-1992 (Permanence of Paper)

1 2 0 4 2 4

Dedicated to Alice Berg, on behalf of her adult art students,
who greatly benefited from her creative encouragement.
She gently unleashed hidden talent in each of us.
We are ever grateful for her generosity in sharing
her wealth of artistic experience with us.

I have a hug to share;

find it almost anywhere.

When you win a race;
feel it as a gentle breeze
brushes your face.

When your day is long;

listen when a wren

sings her song.

When something tickles your nose; it may be the fragrance of a rose.

*When something goes wrong
or doesn't seem right;*

it dazzles in a moonlit night.

When you're
too tired to run;
it glows with
the setting sun.

When you're bewildered and can't find things; it flutters by on gossamer wings.

When you're frightened at night;

it comforts you with the dawning light.

ceil

When you're weak, almost fainting; it holds you in the mystery of a painting.

When you're down and out;

don't pout.

*The bank may be
steep and water wide;*

*I'll help you
to the other side.*

I have a hug to share;

ever present always there.

Like an answer to a prayer:

In the babble of a stream,

Or in the sweetness of a dream.

Be still and look and listen.
Be aware!
A hug is waiting; always there!

www.ingramcontent.com/pod-product-compliance
Lightning Source LLC
Chambersburg PA
CBHW040639100526
44585CB00039B/2871